BROKEN COMMANDMENTS, BROKEN WORLD

A Path Back to God

The Pastor's Children

Scripture quotations are taken from the King James Version (KJV) of the Bible. Public domain.

Broken Commandments, Broken World/ Author Name. -- 1st ed.
ISBN 9798218783297

Dedication

To everyone seeking a path back to God. Take a look at everything happening in the world today. Now is the time to come back to God.

Joshua 24:15 NIV

But if serving the LORD seems undesirable to you, then choose for yourselves this day whom you will serve, whether the gods your ancestors served beyond the Euphrates, or the gods of the Amorites, in whose land you are living. But as for me and my household, we will serve the LORD.

Attend your Bible Study Group at Church or if you are not a member of a church, look for one in your community. If prefer, study your Bible privately. Choose your Path Back to God.

4 · THE PASTOR'S CHILDREN

Contents

INTRODUCTION

The world isn't just broken—it's bruised, bleeding, and boldly calling evil good.

We're watching what happens when humanity rejects the boundaries God gave us for our own blessing. It's not that we've never heard His law—we've simply decided we don't need it.

We **sacrificed** truth for tolerance. Holiness for hype. Conviction for comfort. The result? Confusion in our families. Chaos in our communities. Corruption in our leadership. Compromise in our pulpits.

God's commandments weren't written to crush us. They were given to protect us. They were never about control—they were about a covenant, about forming a people who would reflect His heart to a watching world. But somewhere along the way, we tore down the standard and called it progress.

Now we're raising generations that no longer know what's right—because we no longer preach it. We've silenced the fear of the Lord and turned obedience into a dirty word. Yet we wonder why everything feels like it's falling apart.

But this book isn't just about the diagnosis. It's about the cure. Chapter by chapter, we'll walk through what happens when the commandments are ignored—when love grows cold, when pride replaces humility, when idols are built with likes and platforms instead of gold. We'll hold up Scripture like a mirror and ask hard questions about what we see.

We won't cover every commandment at once. Instead, we'll unpack their relevance—what we've lost by dismissing them and what we can recover if we return. Because this isn't just about law—it's about Lordship. It is not just about rules—it's about relationship.

This isn't just about sin—it's about the Savior who still calls us back. If you're willing to listen—not just with your ears, but with your heart—then this is your invitation. Not to perform or to pretend. But to come back to the God who still speaks.

Before we move any further, it's worth looking at the very words God carved into stone with His own hand. These weren't cultural suggestions or moral options. They were, and still are, the foundation for a life that reflects His character.

Here they are, straight from Exodus 20:1–17 (KJV):
1. Thou shalt have no other gods before me.
2. Thou shalt not make unto thee any graven image.
3. Thou shalt not take the name of the Lord thy God in vain.

4. Remember the sabbath day, to keep it holy.

5. Honour thy father and thy mother.

6. Thou shalt not kill.

7. Thou shalt not commit adultery.

8. Thou shalt not steal.

9. Thou shalt not bear false witness against thy neighbour.

10. Thou shalt not covet.

You'll notice these commandments don't just address behavior—they reveal priorities. They're about who we worship, how we treat each other, and the posture of our hearts before God.

In the chapters ahead, you'll see these commandments woven throughout, not in strict order, but as they confront the sins, struggles, and choices shaping our world today. Some will appear more than once, because sin rarely breaks just one commandment.

The goal isn't just to memorize a list. It's to remember the Lord who gave them, return to the boundaries that protect us, and walk in the kind of freedom only obedience can bring.

CHAPTER ONE

The Fracture: How We Broke It

In the beginning, God spoke a world into being that was whole and good. "God saw all that He had made, and it was very good" (Genesis 1:31, KJV). Creation thrived in perfect harmony—hearts unburdened, relationships unbroken, peace uninterrupted.

Humanity's first task was simple yet sacred: care for the garden and walk in unbroken fellowship with the Creator. No pain. No shame. No separation. Just the way God intended.

But perfection didn't last.

God gave one boundary: "You must not eat from the tree of the knowledge of good and evil, for when you eat from it you will certainly die" (Genesis 2:17, KJV). But Adam and Eve reached anyway. Tempted by the serpent's whisper—"Did God really say…?"—they chose self over surrender. That single act of disobedience cracked open a door for sin to flood the world, and humanity has been living with the fallout ever since.

When we stepped away from God, everything fractured. Families splintered—not just from distance, but from betrayal and generational wounds passed down like heirlooms. Injustice took root, building systems that elevate some and crush others. We see it in racial hatred, human trafficking, political corruption, and the oppression of the vulnerable.

Turn on the news or scroll your phone—chaos screams back at you. Wars in Ukraine and the Middle East. Entire communities displaced by violence and famine. Mass shootings in schools. Innocent lives lost while leaders argue over blame. Truth bends under the weight of influence.

Recent global surveys show less than 20 percent of people worldwide trust their governments to act in the public's best interest, while misinformation spreads faster than the truth. Even the Church isn't immune—too many pulpits trade holiness for popularity, leaving people starving for the Word of God. Beneath it all is greed—a hunger for power, wealth, and control that has replaced reverence for the One who made us.

This is what a broken world looks like.

A creation rewriting truth to suit its desires while the Creator's design sits ignored. Scripture warns: "There is a way

that seems right to a man, but its end is the way to death"
(Proverbs 14:12, KJV). We're living in those days right now.

Yet for all the headlines about moral decay, human kindness
hasn't vanished. People still feed the hungry, hold doors for
strangers, give when disaster strikes. Why? Because the image
of God is still stamped on every human heart (Genesis 1:27,
KJV).

But make no mistake—our kindness alone can't heal what
sin has shattered. The brokenness we see isn't just the absence
of good; it's the absence of God's truth being lived and obeyed.
Until we return to Him, the fracture will only spread.

Still, here's the hope. The same God who made the world
whole is still calling us back.
The One who formed life from dust can rebuild what's been
destroyed.

Sin may have cracked the world, but God never stopped
reaching for it—or for us. From the moment Adam and Eve hid
in shame, He came looking, calling out, "Where are you?"
(Genesis 3:9, KJV). That question still echoes—not as
condemnation, but as invitation.

God has always made the first move toward restoration. He
didn't leave us guessing how to return. Through the prophet
Jeremiah, He promised: "You will seek Me and find Me when
you search for Me with all your heart" (Jeremiah 29:13, KJV).
Centuries later, Jesus declared: "I am the way and the truth and

the life. No one comes to the Father except through Me" (John 14:6, KJV).

No matter how deep the fracture runs—in families, nations, or our own hearts—He offers a way back. The same Creator who spoke life into dust can breathe healing over what sin has shattered.

This book isn't about bad news. It's about God's answer to a broken world. The hope of redemption. The path back to His truth. The life we were always meant to live with Him.

That story isn't finished yet. Every commandment we ignore cracks the world further, but everyone we obey brings us closer to God's original design: order, relationship.

CHAPTER TWO

Love Lost: God's Heart & Man's Hate

From the beginning, God's design was simple: love Him and love each other. It wasn't an emotion—it was a commandment. Love is the heartbeat of God. When we let love rule our lives, the law isn't a burden—it is a blessing. But when love is lost, every other commandment fails.

That's why Jesus said the law hangs on love. The first four of the Ten Commandments show us how to love God—with loyalty, worship, reverence, and trust. The last six show us how to love people—with honor, respect, faithfulness, honesty, and contentment. Love isn't separate from the commandments—love *is* the commandments in action.

But humanity traded love for pride, power, and fear. We see it as early as Cain and Abel. Cain grew jealous when his brother's offering pleased God more than his own. Instead of choosing repentance and reconciliation, he chose rage—and spilled Abel's blood in the field (Genesis 4, KJV). It was the first family fracture, and it revealed what happens when love is replaced with envy and hate.

Even today, we still confuse love with things it was never meant to be. In Greek thought, there were many words for love: **eros** (romantic passion), **philia** (friendship), **storge** (family affection). But the love God commands and demonstrates is **agape**—selfless, sacrificial, unconditional love. The kind of love that doesn't depend on feelings but on covenant.

Agape is the love God has for us—and the love He calls us to extend to each other. When we trade agape for selfishness, every other commandment unravels. We wield "love" to manipulate, control, and even harm, forgetting that true love tells the truth, protects, and restores

Just look around. You don't have to search hard to see that love has been lost. Hatred runs deep—dividing races, classes, and nations. Prejudice hasn't disappeared; it's just found new language and new platforms. Hate crimes against ethnic and religious groups have spiked across the U.S., Europe, and Africa. Families crumble under betrayal, abuse, and generational pain. Violence has become background noise—whether in American schools, or in war zones like Gaza, Ukraine, and Sudan.

Even the Church isn't immune. Denominations splinter. Pulpits echo politics more than scripture. Jesus' own words, "By this shall all men know that ye are my disciples, if ye have love one to another" (John 13:35, KJV), gets drowned out by division.

We've built a culture where anger spreads faster than compassion, where bitterness feels safer than forgiveness. Jesus warned: "Because iniquity shall abound, the love of many shall wax cold" (Matthew 24:12, KJV). That's not some far-off prophecy—it's our reality.

Part of the problem is we've redefined love on our own terms. Love now often means tolerance without truth, or desire without discipline. We celebrate selfishness, mistaking it for freedom, while scorning the sacrificial love God calls us to.

God has always operated from love from the first breath He breathed into Adam to the final breath Jesus took on the cross. He didn't just say He loved us—He proved it.

But we still confuse love with things it was never meant to be. The results are everywhere: shallow relationships, broken communities, unchecked hatred parading as passion—and under it all is a rejection of God. Scripture doesn't sugarcoat it: *"If a man say, I love God, and hateth his brother, he is a liar..."* (1 John 4:20, KJV).

God has never been casual about lies or hate. *"These six things doth the Lord hate: yea, seven are an abomination unto him: a proud look, a lying tongue, and hands that shed innocent blood, an heart that deviseth wicked imaginations, feet that be swift in running to mischief, a false witness that speaketh lies, and he that soweth discord among brethren"* (Proverbs 6:16–19, KJV).

Look closely—that list sounds a lot like the Ten Commandments we've already broken: pride that puts self above God, lies that twist the truth, bloodshed that despises life, coveting and scheming in the heart, false witness that destroys reputations, and sowing division where God commands love. Proverbs isn't inventing something new—it's exposing how abandoning God's law always leads to the same fruit: broken love, broken trust, broken world.

When love is lost, commandment after commandment falls with it. God's love is impartial. It doesn't shift with moods or trends. It's steady, not situational. It's sacrificial, not superficial. It never turns a blind eye to sin—and it never gives up on the sinner.

True love tells the truth, even when it cuts. It corrects without canceling. It protects the vulnerable. It shows up, not to shame—but to shine light in dark places.

Love looks like Christ. It sounds like His words. It moves like His hands. It gives like His cross.

We broke this world because we forgot how to love. Hate divides. Fear distorts. Selfishness destroys. But love—true, godly, sacrificial love—restores what sin has shattered.

Every headline of violence… Every broken family… Every injustice we witness… It all points back to one thing: we drifted from the God who told us how to live. Until we return to Him—the source of love—we will keep destroying what God once called good.

Even in a world where love has grown cold, God hasn't stopped loving us. "For God so loved the world, that he gave his only begotten Son…" (John 3:16, KJV). That wasn't sentiment, it was sacrifice. His love is still the blueprint—and still the invitation.

Through Jesus, we've been given a new command: "This is my commandment, That ye love one another, as I have loved you" (John 15:12, KJV). Not as culture defines it. Not as our wounds distort it. But as He demonstrated it.

The way back is simple, but it isn't easy: Repent of hate. Return to God. Let His love transform your heart. Only then can we rebuild what's been broken. Only then can we love like we were created to. Because only His love makes us whole again.

Love fulfills the law—hatred and betrayal break it. God's command to honor life and relationships still stands.

CHAPTER THREE

The Lie of Human Authority

There was a time when kings trembled before the voice of the prophets. When rulers sought the wisdom of God before making decisions. When power was viewed as a stewardship, not a throne.

But now, pride convinces men they can be their own god—and we bow to human authority as if it were divine, applauding what God forbids. The first commandments warned us: no other gods, no idols, no taking His name in vain. Yet we every time we put human authority above God's authority, we trample those laws. Whether it's a politician, a pastor, or a platform, the moment we bow to charisma instead of character, we trade covenant for counterfeit.

In the Old Testament, Saul was chosen by God, anointed as Israel's first king, and given clear instructions: destroy the Amalekites completely. But he thought he knew better. He spared Agag, kept what God said to destroy, and tried to cover rebellion with sacrifice. Saul still carried the title "king," but God rejected him—not because he lost a battle, but because he disobeyed.

That same spirit is alive today. We follow polls instead of prayer. We measure leaders by platforms instead of purity. We excuse arrogance if it matches our agenda, and we defend corruption if it promises us power. Pride dress itself as progress, but the Word unmasks it: *"Pride goeth before destruction, and a haughty spirit before a fall"* (Proverbs 16:18, KJV).

The lie of human authority is not new. It says, *"You can decide what's right for yourself. You don't need God's authority—you can be your own."* But every time we swallow that lie, commandments crumble, and chaos follows.

We see the fruit of this lie everywhere. Leaders rise to power not because of integrity but because of image. They bully, mock, manipulate, and still get celebrated—sometimes even by those who claim to stand for truth. Charisma gets mistaken for anointing. Popularity gets confused with holiness. And instead of questioning the fruit, we baptize pride and call it leadership.

This isn't just political—it's spiritual. Pulpits have become platforms. Sermons are crafted for applause, not repentance. Too many chase influence without accountability, and the people follow because it's easier to be entertained than convicted. The danger is we start honoring titles more than truth. If someone has a mic or a following, we call it anointing—even if their life denies the God they preach.

But the Word doesn't bend: *"Woe unto them that call evil good, and good evil... that are wise in their own eyes, and prudent in their own sight!"* (Isaiah 5:20–21, KJV). The commandments still stand. God never gave us permission to worship human authority. The first says no other gods before Him. The second says no idols. The third says don't misuse His name. Yet every time we exalt leaders over God, we break all three.

Israel begged for a king, and God let them have Saul. Not because it was best—but because they insisted. Saul's downfall wasn't political—it was spiritual. He feared the people more than he feared the Lord (1 Samuel 15:24, KJV). And we've repeated their mistake. We've followed leaders without discernment, chasing acceptance instead of truth.

But the Word still stands: *"Be not conformed to this world: but be ye transformed by the renewing of your mind"* (Romans 12:2, KJV). Until we stop trying to look like the culture, we will never have the power to change it.

The prophet Micah reminds us of what true leadership looks like: *"He hath shewed thee, O man, what is good; and what doth the Lord require of thee, but to do justly, and to love mercy, and to walk humbly with thy God?"* (Micah 6:8, KJV). That's the blueprint. Not influence. Not ambition. Not performance. Just justice, mercy, and humility before the Lord.

The way back isn't through another election cycle or a viral revival. It's through humility. Through repentance. Through returning to the One whose throne is never up for re-election.

Here's the truth: a person who does not walk with God cannot lead anyone to Him. How can someone point you to truth if they refuse to live under it? How can they call for righteousness when they've already bowed to pride? Jesus said it plainly: *"If the blind lead the blind, both shall fall into the ditch"* (Matthew 15:14, KJV).

These leaders—whether political, spiritual, or cultural—may have charisma. They may speak well. They may gather crowds. But if their hearts are not surrendered to God, their direction will always lead to ruin. You can't take people somewhere you've never been. You can't carry the glory of God if you're more committed to your own name than His.

That's why we keep circling the same chaos. Scandal after scandal. Division after division. Confusion and compromise filling the headlines. We've chosen shepherds who don't feed, kings who don't kneel, and prophets who don't listen.

But this is what happens when we break the very first commandments. When we put other "gods" before Him, when we raise up idols in the form of men, when we misuse His name to defend our agendas—we reap exactly what He warned us against.

Until we stop chasing crowns and start seeking crosses, we'll keep following leaders who are gifted—but godless. Loud—but lost.

Pride and misplaced worship break the foundation of God's law. The first three commandments remind us of who sits on the throne—and it isn't us.

CHAPTER FOUR

Signed in Stone: The Commandments Still Matter

For four hundred years, Israel lived under Egypt's rule. Generations knew the sting of slavery but not the structure of God's covenant. They had God's promises, but not yet His written pattern for living. So, when He brought them out of bondage, He gave them His law—a framework not just for religion, but for life itself.

But while God was giving law, the people were breaking it. Before Moses even made it down the mountain, Israel had already turned their hearts. They gathered gold, shaped it into a calf, and called it their god. They danced. They shouted. They stripped off their self-control and went wild. And when Moses saw it, he shattered the tablets in anger. That moment wasn't just about broken stone—it was about broken covenant.

But even after all that, God didn't toss out the law. He didn't say, "Let's just go with grace and skip the rules." No. He told Moses: "Hew thee two tables of stone like unto the first: and I will write upon these tables the words that were in the first tables, which thou brakest" (Exodus 34:1, KJV). The first set was God's gift; the second came with sweat. Much like Adam working the ground after Eden, Moses had to labor for what was lost. Disobedience always makes the journey heavier.

Nothing has changed. We live in a time where convenience trumps conviction, where people say, "You do you," even if "you" is walking straight into destruction. We've normalized what God calls sin. We ignore the parts that make us uncomfortable. We explain away the commands that demand obedience. We twist His words into loopholes that justify our agendas.

The Word makes it plain: *"The law of the Lord is perfect, converting the soul: the testimony of the Lord is sure, making wise the simple"* (Psalm 19:7, KJV).

The law was never a prison; it was protection. It was never meant to suffocate; it was meant to sustain. God's law was never the problem—our rebellion is. In fact, when we dismiss His commandments, we don't just lose rules—we lose reverence, wisdom, and the very standard that sets us apart.

The commandments weren't just for ancient Israel. They are God's mirror—still revealing what's right, still confronting what's wrong. Not to condemn, but to lead us back. Because a world without God's law isn't free—it's lost.

We've lost honor— children dishonor parents, spouses dishonor covenants, leaders dishonor truth. We've lost rest. The Sabbath has become just another hustle day. No pause. No worship. Just more work, more worry, more burnout.

We've lost holiness—we take the Lord's name in vain not just with curses, but with casualness. We've built idols—not out of gold, but out of status, comfort, money, and self. And the result? A generation overwhelmed by anxiety, drowning in distraction, and starving for something real.

Here is the good news: God didn't just give laws—He gave grace. Not as a pass to keep sinning, but as power to start obeying. Jesus didn't cancel the commandments—He fulfilled them. He said, "Think not that I am come to destroy the law... I am not come to destroy, but to fulfil" (Matthew 5:17, KJV). He lived them perfectly and then died to cover us when we couldn't.

But His death doesn't erase the law—it writes it on our hearts. The way back is repentance. The way back is surrender. The way back is trading our opinions for His truth, our rebellion for His righteousness.

Because when we love Him, we obey Him. Not out of fear, but out of devotion. Jesus said, "If ye love me, keep my commandments" (John 14:15, KJV).

It's not legalism—it's love. It's not bondage—it's belonging.

So come back. Come back to the boundaries that heal. Come back to the truth that saves. Come back to the lawgiver—not for condemnation, but for correction. Not for rules—but for relationship. Because when we return to God's law—we return to God.

God's law is never optional. It still calls us to obedience today.

CHAPTER FIVE

Idols, Images, and Empty Worship

The human heart is an idol factory. If it's not a golden calf, it's a glowing screen. If it's not Baal, it's a bank account. If it's not carved wood, it's carefully curated status. We may not bow down before statues anymore but make no mistake—we still worship what we build.

The second commandment was clear: "Thou shalt not make unto thee any graven image… thou shalt not bow down thyself to them, nor serve them:" (Exodus 20:4–5, KJV). God wasn't being petty. He was being protective. He knows that what we worship shapes us. When we worship what we've created, we become as empty as the idols themselves.

Israel's golden calf wasn't just bad theology—it was broken trust. It was impatience dressed up like religion. They wanted a god they could see, touch, and manage. We also prefer gods we can control. A god who won't convict. A god who blesses our rebellion. A god who looks suspiciously like us.

But idols always take more than they give. They promise power but deliver bondage. They promise freedom but bring slavery. The psalmist wrote: *"They that make them are like unto them; so is every one that trusteth in them"* (Psalm 115:8, KJV). In other words: worship something lifeless, and you become lifeless too. That is not what God wants for His people.

We no longer dance around calves or carve images, but we scroll through feeds and curate brands. Idolatry looks sophisticated now, but we still burn ourselves out chasing the next dollar, the next deal, the next dopamine hit—the same old sin in a new package.

Here's the deeper danger: idols don't just sit on shelves—they sit in churches. When worship becomes entertainment instead of encounter, when sermons chase applause instead of repentance, when leaders build platforms instead of altars—that's idolatry. It may sound holy, but if Christ isn't the center, it's just noise.

Isaiah thundered against this: *"This people draw near me with their mouth, and with their lips do honour me, but have removed their heart far from me"* (Isaiah 29:13, KJV). Jesus echoed it centuries later: *"In vain they do worship me, teaching for doctrines the commandments of men"* (Matthew 15:9, KJV).

God does not want empty worship nor a spectacle and tradition. He wants surrendered hearts. So, what is worship really?

True worship doesn't start with a song—it starts with sacrifice. Paul put it this way: *"Present your bodies a living sacrifice, holy, acceptable unto God, which is your reasonable service"* (Romans 12:1, KJV).

Worship is not about performance—it's about posture. Not stage lights, but a surrendered life. When who we are lines up with who He is, that's worship. This is why the first three commandments matter so much in the conversation about worship.

- *No other gods before Him*—Worship means our ultimate loyalty belongs to God alone.
- *No idols*—Worship means no substitutes, no images, no counterfeits.
- *Do not take His name in vain*—Worship means honoring His name not just with lips, but with lives that reflect His character.

The third commandment ties right in here: *"Thou shalt not take the name of the Lord thy God in vain"* (Exodus 20:7, KJV). Taking His name in vain is claiming His authority while denying His character. It's more than just cursing; it's using His name as a weapon or a cover for our own ambitions, a fraud that leads to society's unraveling when idols rise and His name is misused.

When idols rise and His name is misused, society unravels. Families fracture. Holiness fades. Worship loses weight. Instead of being set apart, we look just like the world.

The call is to smash the idols. Not with hammers, but with repentance. Not by deleting app, but by dethroning self. Not by cursing culture, but by consecrating Christ as Lord in our hearts.

Paul said it this way: *"Little children, keep yourselves from idols"* (1 John 5:21, KJV). It's not just advice—it's survival. Because idols always demand sacrifice, but only Christ gave Himself for us.

The way back isn't complicated. It's the same as it was at Sinai: turn from false gods to the living God. Trade images for intimacy. Trade empty worship for true surrender.

Because the human heart will always build something to bow to. If it's not Christ, it will be counterfeit. But when Christ is on the throne, idols lose their grip. When His name is honored, His presence fills the house again. That is worship. That is life.

CHAPTER SIX

The Power of the Tongue: Lies, Death, and Deceit

Words are never neutral. They build—or they break. They carry life—or they carry death. Scripture doesn't soften it: *"Death and life are in the power of the tongue"* (Proverbs 18:21, KJV). What we speak can heal or wound, set free or chain down, bless or curse.

The ninth commandment was clear: *"Thou shalt not bear false witness against thy neighbour"* (Exodus 20:16, KJV). But this goes far beyond the courtroom. It reaches into our texts, our timelines, our pulpits, and our politics. Every half-truth posted online, every reputation ruined with a whisper, every carefully curated lie we call branding, marketing, or content creation—all of it bears false witness.

We live in a culture where deception has been rebranded. We call it marketing. We call it spin. We call it content creation. But

God still calls it lying. He still hates it: *"Lying lips are abomination to the Lord: but they that deal truly are his delight"* (Proverbs 12:22, KJV).

Lies never stay small. They multiply. They grow fangs. One falsehood demands another until truth is buried under filters, captions, and carefully staged photos. Social media has become a stage where we pretend to be happy, successful, and holy— while our souls quietly bleed behind the screen.

Families collapse under hidden secrets. Marriages break beneath silent betrayals. Churches split when gossip spreads faster than grace. Nations burn when propaganda replaces reality. Satan himself is called *"the father of lies"* (John 8:44, KJV), and every time we twist the truth, we echo his voice instead of God's.

That's why gossip is so deadly. It's not "venting." It's not "just sharing." It's character assassination in disguise. James said it plainly: *"The tongue is a fire, a world of iniquity… it defileth the whole body, and setteth on fire the course of nature; and it is set on fire of hell"* (James 3:6, KJV). In other words: hell has a sound—and it often comes through the human tongue.

The average tongue weighs less than three ounces. It doesn't swing like a sword, but it cuts deeper. It doesn't break bones, but it can crush a spirit. Its size is small, but its capacity for devastation is great.

The danger isn't just "out there." It's us. How often do we exaggerate, cover up, or flatter to gain advantage? How often do we say, "I'll pray for you," with no intention to pray? How often do churches claim growth while hiding sin in leadership? Bearing false witness doesn't just happen in headlines—it happens in our homes, our pulpits, and our hearts.

But God has a remedy. Jesus said, *"Ye shall know the truth, and the truth shall make you free"* (John 8:32, KJV). Lies enslave—but truth liberates. Speaking truth may cost you friends, position, or applause, but it will never cost you your soul. To repent of deceit is to return to freedom. To confess, to walk in the light, to let yes mean yes and no mean no—that is the path back.

The ninth commandment was never about stifling speech—it was about sanctifying it. Our words are meant to reflect the God who spoke creation into existence. If He used His voice to bring light from darkness, how dare we use ours to spread shadows? The call is urgent:

- Stop bearing false witness in your family.
- Stop bearing false witness in your friendships.
- Stop bearing false witness in your worship—when your lips say one thing but your life says another.
- Stop bearing false witness against your neighbor, your brother, your sister, even your enemy.

Paul urged: *"Wherefore putting away lying, speak every man truth with his neighbour: for we are members one of another"* (Ephesians 4:25, KJV).

The way back is not complicated. Repent of lies. Renounce gossip. Speak truth—even when it costs. Because God has not called us to sharpen our tongues like swords, but to use them as instruments of healing, hope, and holiness.

Life and death are still in the power of the tongue. And every word we speak tells the world which kingdom we belong to.

CHAPTER SEVEN

The Covetous Soul: Greed and the Fall of Nations

Coveting rarely makes headlines. It doesn't sound as scandalous as murder or adultery. But God placed it in the Ten Commandments for a reason: unchecked desire is the seedbed for every other sin. It forgets the goodness of God—because it's hypnotized by the gods of greed.

"Thou shalt not covet… any thing that is thy neighbour's" (Exodus 20:17, KJV).

To covet isn't just wanting—it's worshiping what isn't yours. It's fixing your heart on someone else's blessing until gratitude rots and envy takes over. Cain coveted Abel's favor and murdered him. Achan coveted Jericho's spoils and brought judgment on Israel. David coveted Bathsheba and unraveled his own house. From the garden to our news feeds, coveting has always been the spark that ignites destruction.

Covetousness has shaped empires and ruined nations. We see it in politics—policies driven by profit, not principle. We see it in business—corporate greed that exploits workers while CEOs fly private. We see it in culture—where more is never enough, and image is everything. Even churches aren't exempt. We covet influence, platform, and reach. We measure success by followers and funds instead of faithfulness.

But here's what God says: *"Woe unto them that join house to house, that lay field to field, till there be no place…"* (Isaiah 5:8, KJV). Translation? You're stacking and snatching until there's nothing left—and still you're not satisfied. That's not abundance. That's a sickness.

Greed doesn't just poison individuals—it topples nations. When leaders covet power, they trample justice. When corporations covet profit, they exploit the vulnerable. When citizens covet comfort, they trade freedom for convenience. Whole societies collapse when desire outruns discipline.

The tenth commandment was clear: *"Thou shalt not covet… any thing that is thy neighbour's"* (Exodus 20:17, KJV). Coveting isn't just wanting—it's worshiping what isn't yours. It's fixing your heart on someone else's blessing until gratitude rots and envy takes over.

King Ahab wanted Naboth's vineyard. That desire turned into entitlement. Entitlement turned into murder. David wanted Bathsheba. That look turned into lust. Lust turned into lies. Lies turned into death. Judas wanted more than what Jesus offered.

Thirty pieces of silver was the price of his soul. From the very beginning, Adam and Eve had access to everything—except one tree. But coveting twisted the narrative: what God gave wasn't enough, and what He withheld suddenly looked better. That's the lie that still enslaves us.

That lie is costly. We live in a time where people abandon marriages, betray friends, compromise integrity, and sell out truth for the sake of getting what they think they deserve. James captured it perfectly: *"Ye lust, and have not: ye kill, and desire to have, and cannot obtain... Ye ask, and receive not, because ye ask amiss, that ye may consume it upon your lusts"* (James 4:2–3, KJV).

That's the death spiral of desire: Want. Take. Lose. Repeat.

When coveting takes root, it doesn't just cost us stuff—it steals our soul's stability:

We lose **contentment** and peace goes with it. We lose **gratitude** and become blind to God's blessings. We lose **community** because comparison breeds competition. We lose **witness** because we start looking just like the world.

Paul warned Timothy: *"They that will be rich fall into temptation and a snare... and many foolish and hurtful lusts, which drown men in destruction and perdition"* (1 Timothy 6:9, KJV). It's not about money—it's about mastery. Jesus was clear: *"Ye cannot serve God and mammon"* (Matthew 6:24, KJV). One will always win. One will always rule.

So how do we break free? The answer isn't in having more—it's in trusting the One who provides. Paul said: *"I have learned, in whatsoever state I am, therewith to be content"* (Philippians 4:11, KJV). Contentment isn't natural—it's learned. It's the fruit of surrender.

Instead of hoarding—**give**. Instead of comparing—**celebrate**. Instead of envying—**serve**.

Jesus said, *"Take heed, and beware of covetousness: for a man's life consisteth not in the abundance of the things which he possesseth"* (Luke 12:15, KJV).

Your worth is not in your wallet. Your identity isn't in your car, your zip code, your ring, or your résumé. It's in Christ. His blessings are never late. His provision never fails. His plan doesn't require us to scheme, steal, or strive out of fear.

The soul that's content in Christ is the soul that's finally free. Free from comparison. Free from greed. Free from the chains of desire that never satisfy.

But freedom always begins with turning. If coveting leads us into bondage, repentance is what leads us out. The God who wrote His law on stone is still writing His grace on hearts today just as Israel was called to return after rebellion, so are we.

That's where we turn next: what it means to come back—to repent, to restore, to walk again in covenant with the One who never stopped calling us.

CHAPTER EIGHT

Return to the Path: Repentance and Restoration

We broke the commandments. We broke the covenant. But God never broke His promise. From the garden to the wilderness, from Sinai to Calvary—God has always made a way back. He doesn't leave His people in rebellion. He calls. He confronts. He corrects. He restores.

But restoration doesn't begin with noise. It begins with repentance. Repentance isn't just saying "I'm sorry." It's not behavior modification or religious performance. Biblically, repentance means to change your mind—to turn. To stop heading toward sin and start walking back toward God.

It's confession, yes. But it's also realignment. A spiritual U-turn. It's not optional—it's essential. Jesus didn't say, "Try harder." He said, "Repent: for the kingdom of heaven is at hand"

(Matthew 4:17, KJV). When we repent, something happens that religion alone can't produce—restoration.

We want revival. We want healing. We want peace. But we don't want to deal with our sin. We cry out for blessings while still bowing to idols. We ask for breakthrough without breaking our pride.

But the Word is clear: "If my people, which are called by my name, shall humble themselves, and pray, and seek my face, and turn from their wicked ways; then will I hear from heaven, and will forgive their sin, and will heal their land." (2 Chronicles 7:14, KJV)

God's response isn't delayed—it's conditional. He's not waiting on the world to act right. He's waiting on His people to come clean.

Repentance doesn't just cry. It changes. It stops justifying what God condemns. It lets go of bitterness, lust, pride, jealousy, greed. It restores what was stolen. It forgives what was withheld. It tells the truth, even when it hurts.

David didn't just ask for forgiveness after his sin with Bathsheba. He pleaded: "Create in me a clean heart, O God; and renew a right spirit within me." (Psalm 51:10, KJV)
That's the posture. Not defensiveness. Not excuses. Just surrender.

We've broken every commandment. We've mocked His name, bowed to other gods, dishonored His Word, and trampled on His grace. But still—He stands with arms open. Because He is not just a God of wrath. He is the God of return.

"Return, thou backsliding Israel, saith the Lord... for I am merciful... and I will not keep anger forever" (Jeremiah 3:12, KJV). This is the heart of God: not to destroy, but to deliver. Not to condemn, but to cleanse.

Restoration is more than forgiveness. It's wholeness. It's the rebuilding of what sin tore down. The healing of what disobedience shattered.The rekindling of love that rebellion tried to extinguish. It doesn't mean life goes back to how it was. It means life becomes what God intended all along—full of peace, purpose, and presence.

He said, "And I will give them one heart, and one way, that they may fear me for ever... I will make an everlasting covenant with them... I will rejoice over them to do them good..." (Jeremiah 32:39–41, KJV)

This is what we were always meant for: not rule-following, but relationship. Not perfection, but pursuit.

We broke the world when we broke the commandments. We've broken them all—worshiped other gods, made idols, misused His name, profaned His day, dishonored authority, taken life, betrayed covenant, stolen, lied, and coveted. But repentance is the path back and restoration is the promise. God, who is faithful and just, invites us back to truth, holiness, love— back to Him."

God is faithful and just and invites us back. Back to truth. Back to holiness. Back to love. Back to Him. He's not waiting for perfection. He's waiting for humility. He's not asking for performance. He's asking for your heart.

So return. Repent. Restore.

Because the path may be narrow, but it is still open. And the One who carved it with His blood is still calling you home.

Reader Reflection Guide

Use these questions to go deeper, reflect, and respond in prayer or group discussion.

Chapter 1 – The Fracture: How We Broke It

Where in your life have you stepped outside of God's boundaries?

What cracks are showing—and what's the root?

Chapter 2 – Love Lost: God's Heart and Man's Hate

What definition of love have you been living by?

Who do you need to forgive—or love differently?

Chapter 3 – The Lie of Human Authority

Have you placed too much trust in human leaders or systems?

What would submitting to God's authority look like today?

Chapter 4 – Signed in Stone

Do you treat God's Word as sacred or optional?

Where have you picked and chosen which commandments to follow?

Chapter 5 – Idols, Images, and Empty Worship

What "good" thing may have become an idol in your life?

Is God truly at the center of your worship?

Chapter 6 – The Power of the Tongue

Have your words brought life—or damage?

What lies have you believed or repeated?

Chapter 7 – The Covetous Soul

Are you content—or constantly craving more?

Who or what are you silently resenting for what they have?

Chapter 8 – Return to the Path

What does repentance look like in your life?

Where do you need to realign with God's commandments?

Chapter 9 – The Path Forward

How will you begin to live differently because of this book?

What's one commandment you need to revisit and fully surrender to?

ABOUT THE AUTHOR

The Pastor's Children are siblings that grew up in a Christian home surrounded by love. Our parents taught us at an early age the value of fearing God. Our house was always filled with love and laughter. We grew up in a time when homework was done, and you couldn't wait to go outside to play with **all** the kids in the neighborhood until it was dark. We would catch fireflies and put them in jars; play red rover; hopscotch, hide and seek; red light green light, or any made up game that would keep us outside.

Being taught about love and how to love resonates with us today. The purpose of this book is to share with readers the love we were taught to extend to all mankind. We also feel as though God's Love is being ignored and He is not pleased. We hope you find the value of loving God and one another through reading our book.

God Bless You

ACKNOWLEDGEMENTS

To our parents who taught us to live by the one-word God's Commandments echoes today LOVE. Our dad has since passed, but his memory still lives in each of us. He was also a selfless man. The color of your skin, your background or education, did not matter to him. Everyone was treated the same. There was no judgement (because there's only one JUDGE). He did not grow up with much, but in the end, he had all he needed, GOD.

To Mom– a strong filled woman of faith. We are so blessed to call you Mom. You have been there for each of us in different ways and we can't thank you enough for your love and support. Our family is still being led with the same God-fearing faith our dad had before he passed. May God continue to bless and use you to care for people with the same smile you give to us. From the bottom of our hearts, we love you, MOM.

Our Mentor and Life Coach – God has blessed you with a gift to inspire and nurture women. It shows in the positive reviews given in the many works they've created and speaking engagements they attend. Your accomplishments alone are a testament of your amazing talent. God still has plans for your life.